Praise for

Cutting Teeth

Ivan Hobson's *Cutting Teeth* is an ode to the natural world and an elegy for the poet's past: his home, his father: "They taught me / to grind into the millionths, / split tenths on the micrometer; / taught me to play cribbage, / to speak so people could see my eyes." These poems are all heart. And Ivan Hobson has put his heart at risk to write them.

—Jericho Brown, *The Tradition*

I have been excited to watch Ivan's career. He is a thoughtful, attentive, and conscientious poet who brings important ideas to the table and extends the conversation beyond the small confines of the page. His searching eye and open heart reveal so many possibilities for how to love a hurting world.

—Camille Dungy, *Trophic Cascade*

This book is brilliant as a snow globe—with its glowy well-lit family scene: the house, the fence, the tall tall trees—shaken up. Hobson looks back at a quieter time and focuses his gaze, goes granular. It was not that quiet. His gaze is sharp and wise. His heart is strong. History is better because of poets like him. You will be too, when you read this book.

—Kevin Rabas, Poet Laureate of Kansas (2017-2019), *More Than Words*

Cutting Teeth

Cutting Teeth

Ivan Hobson

Meadowlark PRESS
Emporia, Kansas, USA

Meadowlark Press, LLC
meadowlark-books.com
meadowlarkpoetrypress.com
P.O. Box 333, Emporia, KS 66801

Cutting Teeth
Copyright © Ivan Hobson, 2022

Cover & Chapter Art: Earl Thollander
The art in this book has been used with permission of the Thollander estate.

Cover Design: Tracy Million Simmons, Meadowlark Press

Interior Design: Linzi Garcia, Meadowlark Press

Author Photo: Natalie Amaya
Artist Photo: The Thollander estate

POETRY / American / General
POETRY / Subjects & Themes / Places
POETRY / Subjects & Themes / Family

ISBN: 978-1-956578-07-2
Library of Congress Control Number: 2022934736

for Daniel

Publication Acknowledgments

Grateful acknowledgment is made to the following publications, in which most of these poems first appeared:

"Balancing" *North American Review*
"For the Salvation Army" *The Midwest Quarterly*
"Reaching Each Other" *Southern California Review*
"After 99 Years" *South Dakota Review*
"Fourth of July" *South Dakota Review*
"Legacy" *South Dakota Review*
"Summer Job" *South Dakota Review*
"New and Old" *South Dakota Review*
"Hometown" *Flyway: Journal of Writing & Environment*
"Full Moon" *Permafrost Magazine*
"With Dad" *Harpur Palate.*
"From Your Bedroom Window" *Lullwater Review*
"A New Suit for Graduation" *Fourteen Hills*
"Migrations" *Fourteen Hills*
"Labor Day" *Fourteen Hills*
"The Desperate" *The Sierra Nevada Review*
"Staying with Her" *Sandy River Review*
"The Bricklayer" *The Fourth River*
"Cutting His Teeth" *The Fourth River*
"Finding Work" *The Fourth River*
"The First Hammer" *Common Ground Review*
"At the Kitchen Table" *Common Ground Review*
"After Work" *Plainsongs*
"Migrating From Texas" *Plainsongs*
"The Pile" *Plainsongs*
"Our Neighbor" *Plainsongs* and *The Poetry Foundation*
"Danny" *Haight Ashbury Literary Journal*
"Playing Catch (Football)" *Haight Ashby Literary Journal*
"STS-1 (Columbia)" *Aries: Journal of Art and Literature*
"New Mexico" *Aries: Journal of Art and Literature*

"A Waterfront" *Over The Transom*
"At the Fair's Speed-Pitch Booth" *Valparaiso Poetry Review*
"At the Lathe" *Third Wednesday*
"Custody" *The Sow's Ear Poetry Review*
"Dad Told Us the Real Story" *California Quarterly*
"Leaving" *Red Rock Review*
"Local 10" *The Dispatcher*
"Meeting My Future Stepdad" *The City Writes*
"6 p.m." *Third Wednesday*
"On My Seventh Christmas" *Mudfish*
"Our Machine Shop" *Presa*

Personal Acknowledgments

Thank you to the University of Wisconsin-Madison English Department for picking this manuscript to be a finalist for both The Brittingham Prize in Poetry and The Felix Pollak Prize in Poetry.

Thank you to Ted Kooser and The Poetry Foundation for featuring "Our Neighbor" in *American Life in Poetry* (Column 481).

Thank you to Jonathan Hayes for your continued support and sharp editing eye.

A special thank you to Janet, Kristie, Lauren, and Wes Thollander, for sharing Earl's art—it is a joy to be a part of the family.

Thank you to Dan Langton, for whom this book is dedicated.

Poems

I

II

III

IV

I

Provincetown, Cape Cod, Massachusetts

Migrating from Texas
Great Plains Drought 1892

In the cactus blossom night,
wheel iron cools on earth,
canvas lays stretched and roped
over farm tools like a corset
cinched to hide pregnancy.

Around the campfire,
children watch moths flutter,
silver dollars flicked into the air
by men who want to know
who goes first and who goes last.

This is the way they've chosen to come,
hoping to be reborn in California.

The Desperate
for Alfred Zampa

Hundreds of feet below
the girders of the Golden Gate Bridge,
dozens of men wait for work.

They cook beans over open fires,
play cards and talk about the towns
they came from.

Each man waiting for his chance
at a job,

waiting all day for a bridge worker
to quit, get fired, or fall.

The Bricklayer

Jorge's fingerprints have been taken
by the miles of masonry bricks
that have passed through his hands
one at a time,

worn as beach glass is worn—
through the uncounted waves of friction,
through the walls and hedges he builds
to keep things in, or keep things out;

not for the national tides of countries,
but for the ripples of ivy and roses,
the dogs who long to drift
with the moon.

His overalls and beard dusted red,
his boots spotted with mortar,
his three decades across the Rio Grande
without fingerprints.

After Work

When the factory lights are off
and the machines are cold in the night
they do not miss him;

they do not worry when his back is sore,
or when he's late after snow has fallen,

their gears and spindles don't care
about what they catch and try to haul in.

That is for my mother,
at the end of the day

helping him unbutton his work shirt,
whispering into darkness;
pulling him close.

Ivan Hobson

Cutting His Teeth

My son has become old enough
to deny the ballerina
that balances herself
inside his body.

He has taken off his tiara,
stepped out of the caverns
of his mother's heels,

his world now as blue
as the cobalt
stacked in the scrapyard.

I am worried
he will pick up a steel bar,
that his hands
will come away red and wet,
that we will never see her again.

That he will become
like other men in this town,
dusted with the expectations
of the mill,

huddled in the corner of the bar,
swollen with whisky,
afraid to dance.

Our Neighbor

Every family that lived in our court
had an American truck
with a union sticker on the back

and as a kid I admired them
the way I thought our soldiers
must have admired Patton
and Sherman tanks.

You once told me
that the Russians couldn't take us,
not with towns like ours,
full of iron, full of workers tempered
by the fires of foundries and mills.

It wasn't the Russians that came;
it was the contract, the strike,
the rounds of layoffs that blistered
until your number was called.

I still remember you loading up
to leave for the last time,
the union sticker scraped off
with a putty knife,

the end of the white tarp draped
over your truck bed
flapping as you drove away.

Ivan Hobson

Hometown

Most of us tasted rust in our milk,
iron oxide pushed into the pores
of our mothers' skin
by fathers who had come home
from the plant with appetites.

Everything seemed hungry then:
the automated mills and lathes
that were shipped in to hog more,
the bosses who ground their teeth
into calcium carbonate,

our men that bellowed
behind the line
while boxes of strike food
arrived at our doors.

I used to think that red hair
came from mothers who didn't clean
their breasts enough.

I used to know
that the iron we once shaped here
kept us strong.

STS-1
April 12, 1981

When Dad woke me at 3 a.m.,
still in his swing-shift uniform
and smelling like cutting oil,
he handed me a glass of chocolate milk.

On the sofa, snuggled against his chest,
watching Columbia sit
with its nose pointed up
like a hound calling-out the sky.

What could a six-year-old know
about stakes: reassuring Americans,
barking to the Soviets that we
could play fetch among the stars?

There on that Cold War Sunday,
with all those hopes and prayers
Dad roared with the growling fire,
raised me above his head at liftoff.

Ivan Hobson

Great-Grandmother

Our white-haired captain
who navigates cast iron,
steam and flame,
corned beef and cabbage;

our wrinkled Irish ancient
who saves her cooking foil
because of what Uncle Sam
asked for, decades ago.

Tonight the family is at her table,
listening to her prayer
with a piece of communion
in each of our mouths—

she almost lost her top denture
when she paused to smile at me,
and I lost a bit of Christ's body
when I smiled back at her.

Here for Christmas Dinner,
the believers and non-believers
will clutch each other's hands—
say amen.

For the Salvation Army

Through the kitchen window
I watched great-uncle Dick
fishing through our trash,

the dust of The Depression
still inside of him.
Those childhood memories

of saving what could be saved:
cardboard shoes,
butcher scraps in soup,

all those moments
when pride was not a seed
worth watering.

There, on the side of our yard
that tall Topeka Sunflower
up to his elbows

salvaging the old toys
Mom had thrown away
the night before.

Ivan Hobson

Balancing

After mom's layoff
Dad started drawing himself
a bubble bath every Friday night
after his double shift at the plant.

My dad in his bubble bath, drinking
pull-tab beer, listening to the radio,
closing his eyes while trying to forget
the mortgage, the sixty-hour week
he just finished putting in.

I remember the first time I looked
through the keyhole and saw the candles,
saw the way Dad scrubbed the bunker oil
off his face, saw my rubber ducky yawing
in the waves around him

balancing in the candlelight and symphony,
finding a way to stay afloat.

Friction

After Dad pawned
that old sterling teapot,
he didn't say anything,

he just whistled along with Joan Baez
as we drove to the discount grocery store
at the other end of town.

The two of us
picking canned and dried foods,
while Mom a city away

rallied with the workers
at the mouth of the wrought iron gates—
flint in her chant, kindling in her sign.

Garage Sale

You sold Grandfather's tool chest,
socket set, wrenches, cutters.

You sold his hammers, pliers,
the hardhat he let me wear on Sundays.

You sold the rust, the smell of kerosene,
the handles that kept his memory nestled
against my palms.

At the time I didn't need the quarter for the soda,
the dollar for the new toy,

I needed you to tell me that what he built
would always remain.

Dad Told Us the Real Story

Pig paid wolf in cash.
For sale, two prime lots with views.
Inquire at brick house.

Migrations

Near the Pacific Ocean
hundreds of monarch butterflies flutter
in and out of sunshine, the canopy
of the eucalyptus grove around me.

Such a long way from home,
the machine shop being auctioned next month,
the workers that were once so sure
of the iron they milled

finishing the final shift tonight,
pulling up the collars on their wool jackets
and puffing out into the cold.

The full moon will be soft against the wings,
the boot prints left in the snow by the rank and file
before the gates are locked for the last time.

How long have there been migrations?
Families like ours leaving collapsing towns,
fluttering hundreds, sometimes thousands of miles.

So many beings finding, or trying to find, their way.

From Your Bedroom Window

When the midnights became hot enough
to inhale the smell of the tobacco fields
people would drag race down your street—

double shadows of horsepower
rattling your bedroom window.
We used to wait for it,

for those few seconds
when we could peek through curtains
and feel like stars were blazing their paths.

A child's wish on a rural street: to see
winning and losing, what Detroit was building—
these outskirts as the center of something.

II

On My Seventh Christmas

I.

My sisters got makeup kits
and costume jewelry,
I got a .22 rifle
that I told them they could never fire.

In the living room mirror
Dad showed me how to stand,
shoulder, sight; Mom showed them
how to shadow, blend, pucker—

all of us, like fireflies
attracted to our own lanterns
at the water's edge.

At dinner my sisters wore lipstick,
sipped milk through straws
and talked about which movie stars
they would marry.

Somehow I believed them—
believed in the growing distance of current,
the unseen waves pulsing through nerves,
the glow of filaments in vacuums.

After dessert I grabbed my rifle
and marched with Dad to the woodshed,
our breath bright as musket plumes
in the night sky.

II.

Breathe through your nose, Dad said calmly
as I continued to shoot the targets in front of me.
Twice a month we came to this range
where police officers gave me stickers,
trapshooters hi-fived me.

There was no mom here
to scold me about beef jerky,
sodas, chocolate bars.

There was no mom here
to scold me about wild hair,
sunblock, dirty nails—

there was only my father,
a vertebra taller
when anyone asked him my age.

III.

In spring, Dad brought me
to an orchard overrun with ground squirrels,
Son, your bullets have to be snakes now.

I watched dirt mounds through iron sights
and pulled the trigger every time
I saw a rodent stretching into dawn.

Breathe deep, squeeze slowly,
keep your eyes open,
he repeated again and again.

At the tree line we gathered the bodies,
counted the quarters I had earned,
and talked about my future hunting bigger game.

In the silence of the ride home
I thought about the way they sat up to look,
to smell—the way the bullets must have entered
just after the crack of gunpowder reached them.

IV.

At home after I had scrubbed and rescrubbed,
I stood naked and gazed in the mirror
wondering if I could ever
shoulder the weight of a deer rifle.

I lifted one of my sisters' necklaces
from the counter, clasped it around my neck
and thought about the pressure
on diamonds hidden in the earth.

I traced pink lipstick over chapped lips
and wondered about the distance
of current, the unseen waves pulsing
through nerves, the glow of filam—

You almost done in there?

Yeah Dad,
I'm just practicing my trigger pull
and follow through.

Now that's my boy, he said.

Ivan Hobson

Football

When Dad walked in on me
playing alone with Barbie dolls
he stared at me through a long sip of beer
and walked away.

I could hear them in the kitchen:
You're too soft with him—
Well, you don't spend
enough time with him.

The next day Dad came home
with a powder-pink colored trunk,
a chrome heart shaped lock,
and a kid sized leather football.

That evening on the front lawn
the two of us played catch
and practiced tackling.

I wasn't upset
that we missed dinnertime,
or that we ate alone with dirty hands
while watching the Yankees game.

I wasn't upset
that we showered past my bedtime,
or that I used the pumice soap, like Dad,
when I scrubbed my neck and face.

I wish I didn't dream
about my sister's locked trunk,
the dolls and satin dresses
sleeping inside of it;

I wish I didn't sit on those porch steps,
day after day with my football,
waiting for calloused hands to arrive.

Danny

I wasn't invited to Danny's funeral,
but through the kitchen window
I watched my sisters bury him.

A week later,
after watching Frankenstein,
I snuck under the full moon
and dug
for his coffin.

In my bedroom,
I shaved the dog bites
from his plastic arms and legs,

glued his left hand and foot back on,
hooked a 9-volt battery to his head
and painted him green.

The next day
I presented Danny to my sister,
told her how I had saved him.

She said
that she hated zombies,
and so he lived in my room

where it was lonely,
but safe.

At the Kitchen Table

I remember eating cereal
with my dad at dawn
before his shift at the plant.

I remember looking at him
and telling him
that I saw his co-worker Frank
dressed like a woman
in his blue pickup truck last night.

I remember my dad's eyes
big as pig-iron ingots
as he scanned the room
to see if Mom was listening.

I remember him wiping the milk
from his chin with his flannel sleeve
and leaning toward me;

What a person does on their own
is their own damn business,
he whispered in a tone
that taught me the value of a secret
in a small town.

With Dad

In the high-country on horseback
we saw that rattlesnake
get taken into the sky.

What was wrong with the hawk
that it did not finish the job?

The snake striking until it was freed,
falling until it crashed
on the rocks below,

and the hawk drunk with venom
fluttered to the ground
where you told me it wouldn't survive
the afternoon.

There I was, an unsure boy
when I cleared my throat and asked you
if you still loved mom.

Roadside Diner

It was just a stop
between home and the cabin,
between Mom asking him to leave
and a freedom he didn't want.

In cowboy boots and cologne
Dad brushing off sawdust
left in the booth by millworkers
who had come and gone.

The old initials of lovers
carved in the tabletop,
the reflection in the glass window
of what lay before and behind.

That lone waitress pouring his coffee,
a narrow run in her stockings
straight as a flight path from her ankle
into the shadow of her hemline.

Neither of them wanting to believe
in where they were going,
as they looked at each other
and smiled for the moment—

for whatever else was there.

Through the Diner Window

My mom sits
in a red short-sleeved dress
pondering the fractured nail
on her right hand.

My dad,
a wide-jawed man
in a suit and fedora

gazes at the counterman
who's delicately bent
at the sink.

Their entrées have been eaten,
only crumbs and empty coffee cups
are within their reach.

Custody

One night before the divorce was done,
Dad came to my window,

popped the screen and crawled through,
bringing the smell of the swing shift.

He lay on my bed in his factory clothes
curled as though I was a teddy bear.

In the morning there was only me
scrubbing his boot prints away.

Meeting My Future Stepdad

Jarrett didn't show up
with chocolate coins
or compliments for me.

He didn't tell me
I had a quarterback's grip
or say that my drawings
deserved to be hung in the Louvre.

He came smelling like saffron,
wearing a cream colored suit
with a bow-tied bottle of wine
under his arm.

It's nice to meet you, he said
as he followed my mom into her room
and locked the door behind them.

Local 10
for ILWU Members

It is not a shore, scattered
with seashells or swimmers,
but steel cranes and containerships,

workers in overalls and hardhats
hustling what comes in
and lashing what goes out.

It is an American tide, a rhythm
of union brothers and sisters
constant as trade winds.

Whose Waterfront? Our Waterfront!

That was Jarrett's call, to the scabs
caught in the swell.

Cub Scouts

After accepting the award
I was supposed to salute
my dad and stepdad,

but I didn't know who
to look at first,
so I lowered my head
and walked offstage.

Alone in the bathroom, I breathed,
wondered which man to follow,
noticed an eye-shadow case
forgotten by the sink,

and I am not sure
if I saw it as rebellion or escape,
but I traced my fingers
through those metallic colors,

the light sparkling off of skin,
the way it sparkles
off of industrial diamonds
in grinding wheels.

I wonder just how many times
I washed my hands that night,
afraid of what they might see,
of what I had found to admire.

Giant-Octopus Ride

Like my last three birthdays
Dad and I walked at dusk
when we could slither
under the side fence to save admission.

Brushing off the dirt
in the shadows behind the funhouse,
watching the Giant-Octopus
twirl in the sky for the first time;

Bet you don't have the guts, he dared,
before I shook his hand,
before I raised my head
and marched towards it alone.

For twenty minutes I waited in line,
kicking up dust, spitting,
feeling brave as Captain Blackbeard
until the ticket taker told me
I wasn't tall enough.

Ivan Hobson

III

Leverage

When they hurled apples, we struck
by using a 2x6 with a brick fulcrum point
to catapult dog crap onto their lawn,
patio, and into their pool—

Mess with the best, die like the rest,
we screamed as we volleyed
over and over until they retreated.

Cal's mom called my mom,
my mom called Dad,
for ten minutes they were two tomcats
at the same raw bone,

chattering and caterwauling
until Dad pretended the scrap wasn't worth it.
You're right, I'll change our plans, he said.

> At dawn, Dad woke me,
> *If you still want to go to the fair*
> *then go quietly to the car,*
> he whispered before he grabbed
> my uniform and snuck away.

> On the drive he explained,
> *The note says, I'm taking you*
> *to the Cub Scout Clean-Beach-Drive,*
> *says it's a fitting punishment,*
> *now, if we don't stick to this—*

I'll stick to it, I swear.

Inside the fair,
Dad bought me a candied apple
and a carton of milk.

I ate slowly, chewing my odds:
the way Mom could often sense truth
from eyes and smiles, the way
she could ask questions to free it,

but I knew what men like Dad could do
when they needed to be stealthy
as king snakes.

       Sneaking us past the dirt track,
       unseen to the pits, where the gangs
       of men were tinkering and tuning
       big American cars.

       Dad walked me around,
       asked drivers if they would sign my shirt;
       all of them—stars with a felt tip marker.

       The derby was friction, leverage,
       luck in mud; gear teeth and iron revolting
       over and over until the #141
       was the only car that moved.

       On the drive home I changed
       into my uniform, dusted my shoes
       and pockets with the sand Dad had brought.

Ivan Hobson

At home while I soaked in the tub
Mom came in with fresh clothes,
startled when she lifted my tank top
and saw the signatures.

*Did all the cub scouts sign their names
and troop numbers on each other's shirts?*
I pretended I didn't hear her,
just sunk my head deep under the water.

The Pile

It started with a 5% pay cut, the strike,
the clumsy scabs who produced junk,
the scab inspectors who okayed
and allowed shipments.

The biggest returns came by freight,
weekly until a nest of metal
laid rusting out in the yard.

The concessions were too late,
the reputation of quality was gone,
the ironworks closed the day I was born.

I learned to keep my birthdate from the old-timers,
it was an inward look
like the reflection of a razor nicked throat
that I hated seeing in those men.

Dad did okay though,
he and some of the other guys
were taken in by the tractor plant.

For over five years we played army
and stickball around that rust pile,
but I never saw any kid go in.

We had our own taboos.
You never wanted to stand
where your mother or father
had been let go.

Ivan Hobson

After 99 Years

There was no strike at the tractor plant,
just a deadline when the workers
who once claimed to have yellow paint
in their veins, had to be gone for good.

Dad made it out okay,
buying machines at auction,
moving into his grandfather's workshop,
heading out into business alone.

But what did I know of this city
struggling to find itself?
With industry built over farms,
with its mighty Caterpillar slinking away.

In the Machine Shop

I take a light cut, trying to keep
the chatter down, but the steel part
still whistles like Mother's kettle at dawn.
It is early to be here,

with these controls to move and remember,
with my father who has been waiting
to pass down his craft—now standing back
to let me inherit my own mistakes,

the confidence
to move the lathe carriage without fear,
to create the long helical chips
that come from seasoned hands.

It is here that I will learn to grind
a mirror finish in steel,
that I will get to see those lost reflections,
the old ways of Grandpa teaching Dad.

Ivan Hobson

The First Hammer

Near the old milling machine
there's a copper-headed mallet
with the name *Abel*
branded on both sides.

In this machine shop
there is no one to claim it,
or give it back to,
just two Ivans, father and son.

As a boy
I knew whose mallet it was:
faces scarred and seasoned as relics,
its handle worn as the hooves of his herd.

That long lope of childhood
when the tools weren't meant for work,
when my imagination was free
and unwilling to lie down.

Summer Job

On Saturday, I used diamonds
to dress forms in grinding wheels,
the ground silica like plumes
of musket smoke in winter.

I told them I was 18,
but they all knew
they could make me qualified;
these men who knew my dad,

who called each other *Colonial*
after the white industrial dust
that powdered hair and faces.
They taught me

to grind into the millionths,
split tenths on the micrometer;
taught me to play cribbage,
to speak so people could see my eyes.

Leaving with that long rusty sunset,
wearing a tri-cornered hat,
their tradition for those who retire.
Fifty years too young.

But there in the outskirts, in the town's
last commercial machine shop,
they knew how I felt,
what it meant to me to belong.

Ivan Hobson

A New Suit for Graduation

You're the first of us, my dad tells me
as he leans on the tailor's counter
unfolding a stack of twenty-dollar bills
worn and soiled as his swing-shift fingers;

as if he was my grandfather
leaning on his welding bench
sweating pipe at the shipyard before dawn;

as though he was my great-grandfather
leaning on his plow handle
while inches of Kansas blew away.

A Waterfront

When I drove Grandpa to his hometown
he explained O'Shea's Seafood Grotto,
Pierre's bait and tackle shop,
the way hand-processed fish
and saltwater used to smell at dawn.

*For five decades I have been scared
to come back here*, he mumbled
as though he had snapped the line
but kept the hook.

6 p.m.

Most of my friends can remember
the way their bodies folded at dinnertime,
the way their little eyes fell
after their fathers hung up the phone
to tell them the tractor plant was dry.

All those calls across town,
rank-and-file to rank-and-file;
Dad unplugging the phone to eat in silence.

A butterfly just outside our door,
wind gusting against its wings
until it fell like a playing card
dropped by a beaten hand.

It did what our families would learn to do,
it got up and kept on living.

IV

Old Bone in the Flower Bed

The grip of midnight,
when I woke to my own shallow breath,
hound-eyed and tight-jawed.

The ring I once gave you,
now resting on my nightstand,
dull from years of drift.

What dogged fortune
have I awoken in this moonlight,
these memories I can't surrender?

What luck is it,
that today I dug up the ring
you lost in the garden so long ago?

Leaving

I drove east past midnight,
Ferris wheel lights,
boutiques and restaurants
built where industry once exhaled,

past where I was born,
the bowling alley where my dad
first notices my mother's eyes;

from the highway ridge
it all looked like fireflies
scattered in summer.

By 3:00 I was where I had never been—
wheat fields near pumpjacks drawing oil,
the long stretch of power lines humming,

a convoy of diesels rumbling,
single file with hood emblems
bright as angels against the night.

Ivan Hobson

Chihuahuan Desert

This hard desert between us,
spotted with ghost towns,
with dust and sand that covers
the tracks of things that have been.

Maybe we could have started over here:
in this middle,
where there are more stars than city lights,
where the night is barren enough
for two people to orbit each other.

Reaching Each Other

How long have we been coyotes
on top of our own mesas
barking into the night?

Letting our friends,
curious as echoes,
bounce our lives between us.

It is a canyon formed from pride:
ice that cut through our footing
to make the walkable not walkable.

There is always the heart,
but those are the wings
the two of us seem most afraid of.

Ivan Hobson

Staying with Her

I wouldn't look for a machining job here:
the streets too narrow, dust on cars too thin,
too many boutiques; too many manicured hands,
fingernails clean and smooth as machined delrin.

Janelle bought me a suit,
created my resume—stretched facts
for bank, office, sales managers.

At the interviews I shook their hands quickly,
nervous of the truth in my palm—the pads
of hardened skin, scar tissue of mistakes.

Nervous of my stiffness in dress shoes,
my distrust of neckties because of what power
and moving parts could do if they caught them.
Of the few that said they would—no one called back.

Finding Work

The unemployment office
sent me to Crème de la Crème,
women's shoes and accessories.

I worked the back,
sorting and stacking inventory,
running sizes for saleswomen.

I should have hated it,
but there was something in the stitching,
the precise intervals of thread
that ran along buckles and seams;

something in the geometry of weight;
the curves and tapers of archways and heels,
the bound layers of materials too soft
for carbide to force into tolerance.

There were inventory nights
when I was alone on the sales floor
washed in the precision and color;
where I wondered what it would be like
if my hands and feet were like theirs.

Ivan Hobson

Full Moon

There came a day
when no one asked where I was from,
when I realized that my accent
had become like your accent

and instead of whispering to you
in the bed that night,
I lay silent, overtaken by a dog
howling in the distance.

I have read that it is all just a myth,
that the moon and dog have nothing
to say to each other,

but I am not so sure.

Reunion

Dad and I had talked, but I hadn't seen him
since the fall. At dusk I pushed him, laughed
as he joked about sneaking in for my birthday.

Inside the fair we ate deep-fried crab,
drank beer, looked over vintage tractors
set up where the go-carts used to run.

Waiting in line for the Ferris wheel,
that red-haired boy in front of us
clinging to his father's hand
the same way I used to cling to mine.

How did we get from there to here,
to me looking after him?

Helping from wheelchair to ride cabin,
the two of us shoulder to shoulder
looking out on the town.

In this orbit our speed is the same,
it is our velocity that's changing.

Ivan Hobson

The Patriot

Outside the factory, the old-timer in overalls
shakes my hand hard like his father once taught him to do
and tells me it's a good day to be an American.

It's reassuring to feel that Yankee grip,
one that pulled PRR power lines during The Depression,
that clutched a rifle on the beach at Normandy,
that squeezed a rosary as Apollo 11 lifted off.

Tonight he is handing us po-boys and coffee,
he is getting us ready for the scabs
who will come at dawn to test our line.

Fourth of July

The retired shop steward sits
wearing his service medals,
telling Dad
about the Maginot Line,

the fabrication shops
and shipyards that rallied
for the war.

Telling him about the Midwest:
the tug-of-war with China
over production and fire.

There in the twilight,
all those decades of steel
flickering on his tongue,

molten and heavy,
until the cool night bloomed,
until the flashes and reports
silenced him from the sky.

Ivan Hobson

Flint

He told me the automotive plant
his uncle retired from
took him right out of high school
and five years later let him go.

Last in, first out,
the way many of the workers went
as production left the country
and I left the state.

He said the day he got to California
he stood on the coast watching the sunset,
his shadow long as blocks of parked Buicks
that would no longer be built back home.

New Mexico

My nephew and I limp
into Deming, into a drive-thru
bright with florescent lit moths
wobbling in orbit.

He is excited to fetch sodas
from a teenage girl on skates,
to pass me tools from palms
pale and devoted as moons.

I want to tell him about gravity,
about the pull of his desires,
to watch her, to follow his father
and I into machining.

I want to tell him that he doesn't
want the weight of the blue sky
around his collar; that calloused
fingers are not rocket ships.

Ivan Hobson

Legacy

In the empty sardine can of the 1930s
Great-Granddad ghosted a riverbank
each midnight/midday
bloomed moonshine
hidden in the cross sticks,
cat tail, and thickets;
enough to save family land.

In the pig iron anniversary of the new millennium
the still sleeps in the attic of the machine shop
disassembled and rusting in mouse-chewed burlap sacks.

On my birthday, Dad dusts off
the last ancient vessel of lightning,
a gallon jug holding less than a quarter inch.

On the back porch we each take a thimble sip;
Dad whistles in thru his teeth to cool his throat,
mumbles at the corn moon,
then tells me that I have become the type of man
who will always know how to make more.

Labor Day

In the hotel pool at sunset
I saw a dragonfly
still on the water's edge.

I offered my finger as a raft,
waded the two of us towards the sagebrush
just outside the shallow end.

When I was young my fingers knew
they were meant for threading needles,
untying small knots, touching my mother's face.

They understand metal now, machine dials,
nicks from lathe chips and grinding wheels.
They have grown used to force and friction.

They are no longer scared to save the drowning,
to hold and set the spiders free outside the door.
There is nothing they want to harm.

They are just not as nimble.
Offering the safety of a branch,
accidentally tearing a wing.

Ivan Hobson

At the Lathe

When the steel bar is turning
and the carbide insert is cutting
what I have asked it to cut,

the metal shavings can spin off
fine as piano wire.

Will you play for me tonight?
Something gentle as a butterfly,
your eyes on our wedding?

Help me forget these machines,
all painted gray with their different
ways of friction, and voices

like factory workers
at a bar near closing time.

Play for me tonight my love,
remind me I am delicate,
something silk underneath it all.

New and Old
Oakland-San Francisco Bay Bridge

I sharpened tools for bridge workers
who made me grit my teeth
when I saw them walking on catwalks
steep as horns, hundreds of feet
above where butterflies would flutter.

It reminded me of the wind,
what it takes to be sure of foot, safety tethers,
the way fog on steel becomes unruly as ice.

On Labor Day the new bridge opened
while the old one waited
quiet and patient as rust.

Where is the memorial for those first builders,
for the two dozen who lost their lives?
For the riveter who hit the water flat,
floating with his clothes torn open
and his eyes reflecting the sky?

Ivan Hobson

At the Fair's Speed-Pitch Booth

The batter and catcher are nothing more
than dim silkscreens on a canvas backstop,

but when the baseball hits at ninety-two
there is a snap that makes me want it to be real:

to see this young man on a mound, far
from his work boots, whatever job he has

that gave him the scar on his shoulder,
shaped like the toe of a horseshoe.

Let him be lucky enough—to have lights
brighter than this midway,

to have more than just me, watching the fire
he hurls into the belly of the night.

Bumblebee

You didn't fly into this machine shop
and anoint my lips like Plato or Pindar,
instead you circled the turret lathe
and landed on my chin.

It is foolish to think
that you are the one I saved
from the chip pile last night,

but I am foolish, and why else
would you have come here
sure as a thankful friend?

It is right for me to trust you,
to believe that we are both just workers
and poets curious about each other.

There are steel and flowers
waiting in the pause we take.
There is your ancient song,
as you flit away to the fields at dawn.

Our Machine Shop

This is where I come to meet you;
in the ancestral weight of tool handles,
in the steel dials polished down
by decades against your palms,
in the anvil you brought from Texas
after the family farm went dry.

This is where I can feel you around me;
after the windows have become glazed
with darkness, after the iron in the air
has grown thick on my tongue
and I am working alone.

There are times I stand the way
you must have stood, swaying tired
on the balls of my feet,
biting metal with stronger metal;

times when I hunch the way
you must have hunched, grinding tools
between centers while the spirit
rides the sparks.

This is where I leave the photographs,
where I walk where you walked
before I was born.

This is how I've come to know you;
the grandfather I was named after,

the son my great-grandmother
misses each night.

This is where I trust you;
where I unwrap my whispers,
the fragile wings I keep hidden
from the world.

This is where I confess
when I don't know how to mend
delicate things.

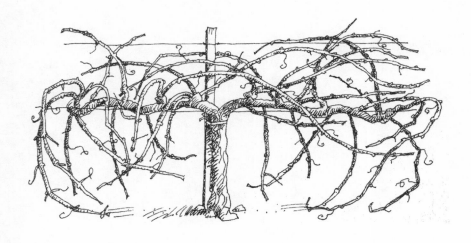

About the Author

Ivan Hobson is an MFA graduate from San Francisco State University. Along with teaching English at Diablo Valley College, he works as a shipyard machinist in Alameda, California. Ivan's poems have appeared or are forthcoming in publications, including the *North American Review*, *Hunger Mountain*, *The Midwest Quarterly*, as well as Ted Kooser and The Poetry Foundation's *American Life in Poetry*.

About the Artist

Earl Thollander was a Californian artist, illustrator, and author who is best known for his painting, sketching, and travel book writing. Earl earned his bachelor's degree from the University of California, and later attended San Francisco Art Institute and the Academy of Art.

Earl had a great interest in traveling and started making artwork that related to the different parts of the world he visited. He became renowned for his unique drawing and painting style, often exploring the Napa Valley. In his career, Earl authored and illustrated more than 62 travel, cooking, and children's books, including *Back Roads of California*, *Earl Thollander's San Francisco*, *School for Julio*, and *Sunset Cookbook*.

Meadowlark POETRY

Books are a way to explore, connect, and discover. Poetry incites us to observe and think in new ways, bridging our understanding of the world with our artistic need to interact with, shape, and share it with others.

Publishing poetry is our way of saying—

We love these words,
we want to preserve them,
we want to play a role in sharing them
with the world.

Meadowlark Press
— since 2014 —

meadowlark-books.com